Tyrannosaurus

Written by Angela Sheehan
Illustrated by George Thompson

Library of Congress Cataloging in Publication Data

Sheehan, Angela.
  Tyrannosaurus.

  Includes index.
  SUMMARY: Describes in text and illustrates a characteristic day in the life of Tyrannosaurus as he searches for prey to assuage his hunger.
  1. Tyrannosaurus rex—Juvenile literature.   [1. Tyrannosaurus rex.   2. Dinosaurs]   I. Thompson, George. 1944-   .   II. Title.
QE862.D5S466   1981   567.9'7   81-109
ISBN 0-86592-114-8   AACR1
(0-8167-1305-7 trade ed.)

Watermill Press
Mahwah, New Jersey

Brontosaurus
(Apatosaurus)

Pteranodon

Dimetrodon

Cetiosaurus

Iguanodon

Stegosaurus

Tyrannosaurus

Tyrannosaurus

Triceratops

Parasaurolophus

Ornithomimus

Ankylosaurus

Tyrannosaurus slowly rose up on his huge hind legs and threw back his head. His sleep had been disturbed and he was angry. A little mammal, catching dragonflies in the ferns, had scampered over the sleeping giant's head. Now the tiny creature clung fast to a dead branch on the ground. His hair stood on end while the meat-eater searched him out.

Suddenly the breeze carried the bellows of duckbills up from the misty hollow, and Tyrannosaurus forgot his rage. He turned his head to listen to the dinosaurs, and the little mammal dropped to the ground and fled into the myrtle scrub.

Tyrannosaurus was hungry. The sound of the duckbilled dinosaurs made him feel even hungrier. He strode off in search of them. Every other creature fled as he moved through the thick undergrowth. Birds flew up before him and lizards darted out of his way.

As he marched the sky grew dark. Thunder rolled through the hills and rain poured from the black clouds. Branches bent and cracked under the force of the downpour. Tyrannosaurus pounded onwards, careless of the driving rain. But there was no chance of him catching the duckbills now. The thunder drowned their bellows and he was still too far away to pick up their scent.

By the time the storm had cleared, Tyrannosaurus was far beyond the woody hills. Ahead of him far across the plain he spied a herd of Triceratops. They were grazing on the warm, wet ferns that covered the sunlit ground. With no trees to hide him now, he had to move carefully. His prey must not know he was coming.

The hunter slowed his pace. Only the sound of his clawed feet rustling through the ferns could be heard. But that was enough. One Triceratops caught the sound and roared a warning to the rest. The animals bunched together in a tight mass of armor.

Only one animal was unable to reach the safety of the herd. She stood in the great reptile's path as he approached. She saw his sharp teeth flash in the sunlight and felt the ground shake as he began to thunder towards her.

At the last moment she wheeled and charged him. Her heavy body crashed into Tyrannosaurus and her sharp horn tore into his thigh. He bellowed with pain and limped away bleeding.

Tyrannosaurus was not only hungry now, but tired and hurt as well. He could not chase the Triceratops, so he rested for a while and then stirred himself again to look for food. He headed back to the valley. At the edge of the swampy river a clump of maidenhair trees grew. Feeding on these was a group of duckbills; and farther along the shore was a flock of pink wading birds.

The noise of the birds made it impossible for the duckbills to hear the dreadful tread of Tyrannosaurus. They went on eating. Then Tyrannosaurus charged, trailing blood from his aching thigh. The birds rose into the air like a pink cloud, their wings clattering. Without looking, one duckbill crashed into the water and swam for his life. The others followed it, struggling to reach the safety of the deeper water. Tyrannosaurus raged along the bank. He was too heavy to cross the swampy ground. There was no way for him to reach his prey.

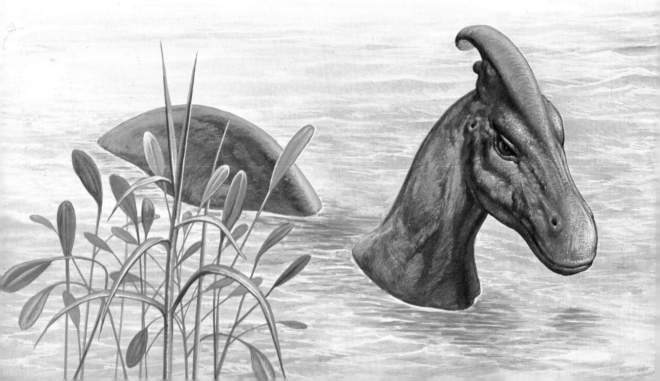

For hours Tyrannosaurus prowled along the high ground by the edge of the river. A crocodile watched him from the opposite bank. Marsh turtles and terrapins plopped into the water as he passed. A pterosaur glided by and he lunged at it. But his great jaws snapped on empty air as the leathery wings brushed past him.

The sun dropped and a cool wind blew. The wind made the wound on the reptile's thigh sting with pain. Now he was too tired to hunt, so he limped to a clearing in a nearby redwood grove. There he stretched out on a soft bed of plants and went to sleep.

Tyrannosaurus slept peacefully. With nothing to fear from the sleeping giant, the other animals crept from their hiding places to hunt for food, or settled down themselves to sleep through the night.

Long after daybreak, Tyrannosaurus was still asleep. The morning chorus of birds was over and the

plant-eating dinosaurs had long been munching the
dew-sodden plants. They were well hidden by the giant
green fronds of the ferns, so Tyrannosaurus did not see
them when he woke. His leg was stiff and sore. It hurt
when he walked, but he could not afford to rest any
longer. He must find food.

He headed for the river again. On the way he
heard a harsh scraping noise coming from behind some
rocks. As quietly as he could, he looked over a crag and
then let out a roar. Just below him was a Struthiomimus.
The long-legged dinosaur was scraping the sand from
a nest of new-laid eggs.

It had just smashed the shell of the first egg
when Tyrannosaurus roared down on it. The dinosaur
darted away, over the rocks into a dense grove of
palms. Tyrannosaurus had no chance of catching the
nimble creature. Once again his prey had escaped.

So Tyrannosaurus skirted the grove and continued towards the river. He could already smell the water when he saw before him the backs of a herd of alamosaurs. Their necks stretched high into the topmost branches of the trees. Some distance from the herd stood a young one, all on its own. It was busy eating fig leaves.

Tyrannosaurus raced forward. His great clawed hind foot slashed into the young dinosaur's body and his teeth sank into the back of its neck. The young Alamosaurus crashed to the ground, lashing its tail helplessly under the killer's weight. The other alamosaurs bolted away, as Tyrannosaurus ripped hungrily into his victim's flesh.

When Tyrannosaurus had gorged enough, he staggered away, bloated and drowsy. What remained of his victim's corpse was not left alone for long. The birds that had circled overhead while Tyrannosaurus ate his fill now swooped down to take their turn. And two scavenging dinosaurs darted in to seize a share of the feast. Tyrannosaurus walked back up the cliff. He was now no danger to any animal, though none was brave enough to approach him. He found a sandy hollow, sheltered by a tangle of magnolias. Here he lay down to sleep off his meal. The little reptiles and mammals that lived in the hollow kept well clear of the giant. When he woke he might be hungry again.

Tyrannosaurus and the Cretaceous World

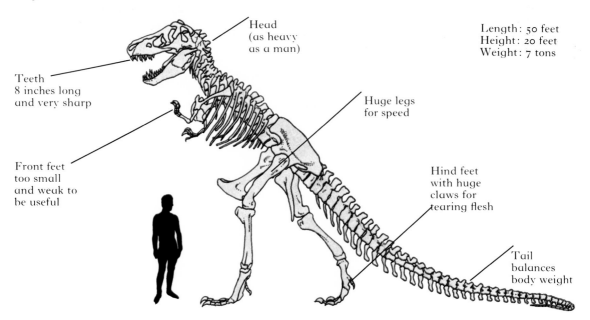

Head
(as heavy
as a man)

Length: 50 feet
Height: 20 feet
Weight: 7 tons

Teeth
8 inches long
and very sharp

Huge legs
for speed

Front feet
too small
and weak to
be useful

Hind feet
with huge
claws for
tearing flesh

Tail
balances
body weight

The skeleton of Tyrannosaurus compared in size with a man

The Age of Dinosaurs

The Mesozoic Era, or Age of Dinosaurs, was divided into three parts: the Triassic, Jurassic and Cretaceous periods. When Tyrannosaurus lived, about 90 million years ago, the Age of Dinosaurs was coming to an end and the world was changing.

During Jurassic times, the plants were mostly ferns, conifers and palm-like plants called cycads. In Cretaceous times there still were many conifers, but there were also flowering plants. Today there are more flowering plants —from daisies to big oak trees—than any other kind. But in Cretaceous times these plants were new. Two of the earliest kinds were magnolia and myrtle.

The Prehistoric King of Beasts

Tyrannosaurus was the largest flesh-eater ever to walk on earth and the master of his world. Running on his huge back legs, he leant forwards and his great tail balanced the weight of his body. He brought down his prey with the sharp claws on his hind feet and killed it with his dagger-like teeth. His front legs would have been no help in a struggle. They were ridiculously small with only two clawed toes on each. Tyrannosaurus may have used them to steady himself as he rose from the ground, or he may have used them as tooth-picks.

Attack and Defense

Tyrannosaurus was big enough and fierce enough to kill any animal. But first of all he had to catch his prey—and few animals allow themselves to be caught easily. Even the most peaceful have some form of defense, such as an ability to outrun or hide from the attacker, or weapons and armor to fight with. Most of them also live in herds which gives them more safety. A hunter is far more likely to attack an animal on its own than with others, and also there are more animals to give the alarm when danger threatens.

Like an elephant with a lion, the sheer size of Alamosaurus was enough to deter an attack. So Tyrannosaurus would not normally have tackled one unless it was so young or so old that it could not fight back (see page 19). An adult Triceratops (see page 8), weighing as much as eight tons, could also protect itself.

Perhaps the easiest prey for Tyrannosaurus were the duckbilled dinosaurs (hadrosaurs). These plant-eaters were a little smaller and much weaker than Tyrannosaurus. The strange "crests" on their heads looked like helmets or horns, but they were not in fact used for defense. The crests were connected to the nose: they may have helped the animals pick up an enemy's scent more quickly or made their bellows sound louder. Apart from that, the duckbills' only real chance was a swift dash, or the kind of lucky escape they had on page 11.

The plant-eaters did not only have the big meat-eaters to fight. There were many smaller ones. These could not kill them, but they could do them harm. Struthiomimus (see page 16) and the scavenging Ornitholestes (see page 20) would probably both have eaten the eggs of other dinosaurs and perhaps their young as well. The little mammals that lived in Mesozoic times may also have eaten dinosaurs' eggs.

In the Air

Nobody knows much about the birds that lived during Cretaceous times. Scientists think that they must have been much like the birds we know today. The wading birds on page 11, for example, were probably like modern flamingoes. The birds could fly well so they had few enemies to fear. The flying reptiles, the pterosaurs, could not really fly. They lived near seas or lakes and glided over the water, picking up fish and insects (see page 13).

The Death of the Dinosaurs

Tyrannosaurus and his giant relatives were among the last of the dinosaurs. At the end of the Cretaceous period, about 70 million years ago, they all died out. The Age of Dinosaurs was at an end. The little mammals grew bigger and bigger. Today mammals are the most important animals. What killed the dinosaurs? Nobody knows, for certain, but most scientists think that the world grew too cold for them. Only animals with fur or feathers (mammals and birds) could survive the cold.

Picture Index

Apart from Tyrannosaurus, these are some of the other animals that you can see in this book:

Things To Do

Try to think of modern animals that are like the dinosaurs in this book. Tyrannosaurus was fierce like a lion. Can you think of any plant-eaters like the duckbills or like Triceratops?

Tyrannosaurus lived long before there were any people to see him. So we can only guess what he was like by looking at his skeleton. The artist who illustrated this story made him brown. Paint a picture of him and the other animals in the colors you think they might have been.

Make a model of Tyrannosaurus and the other animals, with modeling clay. You can use long-grain rice for Tyrannosaurus's teeth and claws.

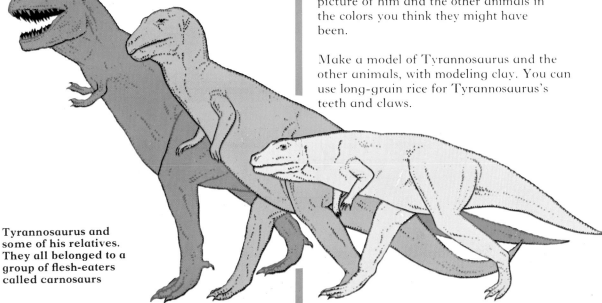

Tyrannosaurus and some of his relatives. They all belonged to a group of flesh-eaters called carnosaurs

Tyrannosaurus Allosaurus   Megalosaurus